Stories
&
Sins

Kenneth Dolan Briodagh

Copyright © 2020 Kenneth Dolan Briodagh

All rights reserved.

ISBN: 9798665364834

StoryPhoenix

This is for my loves. Daniel, Vanessa, and Laura.
You are all inside me and inside this book.
You give me stories and love my sins. Thank you.

The blow

Eagle beats his wings above a blizzard,
Four centuries cold, an aeon old,
Eagle owns the skies above the hunkered.

He flies blind to the storm and its murdered,
Screeches that nature is his to hold,
Eagle beats his wings above a blizzard,
To overlook the still frozen interred.

Smug, he hunts. Sure, kills hundredfold, cold.
Eagle owns the skies above the hunkered.

He soars over cities of beleaguered,
bedraggled, benighted, burning, sold.
Eagle beats his wings above a blizzard
That frosts amber fields, leaves them disfigured,
Painting the purple mountains white-gold.

Eagle owns the skies above the hunkered
But the hunkered are hungry to be heard,
Burning the streets and Eagle's strongholds.

Eagle beats his wings above a blizzard,
Eagle owns the skies above the hunkered,

But they build a fire, in the stone cold,
A fire to warm them, break through the numb
There must come a time to free the controlled.

Eagle calls their fire danger: Behold
how you burn your homes, are misbecome.

But they build a fire, in the stone cold,
Raccoons and Possums and Ravens hold
Meetings and marches, not to succumb.

There will come a time to free the controlled,

Cry out the creatures at Eagle's scold.

Blizzard freezes us, and you're benumbed,
We will build a fire, in the stone cold.

Eagle spies Raven, her words hot, gold:
Burn, cajoles Raven, thrum and beat drums,
Time at last has come to free the controlled.

The Possums bring heat to the streets,
                                    and Raven knows she's been heard
The Raccoons free the frozen imprisoned,
                                    and all can behold
what comes of blizzard smothering:
                                    it becomes un-forged freedom.

Eagle beats his wings against the blizzard,
Eagle cedes the skies to ease the hunkered,
They will tend the fire, against stone cold,
For now is the time to free the controlled.

Voice

There is a voice inside my head that cries out from the wilderness like a headless baptist who needs just water, grasshoppers and threads to exist. And thread is a luxury to yearn for, not more. And I call back to the voice to present ID or something and it says to mind my own business, but that I'm too proud. And I don't think I believe it. But I'm trying and if I try hard enough I think I'll convince myself to buy into the grasshoppers and water from cacti three meters high and their exterior spigoty prickle arms. I don't know if I'll ever be able to look for the head, though. That is too much. Especially since I know I won't get it. At least somewhere in my mind I do.

Storm

Quiet and dawn
Calm and soft sounds
Soon animals stir;
Flowers awake
To the warming sun.
Then
The peace is broken.
Sundered by the thunder of
the Dragon

Its acreage of wings blot out the sun
Brimstone breath searing to earth
Creatures run. Run,
Run for the safety of caves and holes
Flowers close.
All this while the Dragon circles.
Soon but not enough, the beast wings away

The wild creatures creep out of homes and burrows
The flowers slowly open fragile petals to the sun
It is easy now to frolic, forgetful
All calm and quiet.

Walkingstory

As I walkatop the remains of cliffs,
I hear a story filled with broken, jagged edges
that give mute testimony to a sundering.

I imagine a giantsaxe lopping away the land,
Maybe to make room for a palace. Or to kill a pirate.
Either way, it fellaway at the lochaber's swing.
Now gulls roostandlay and seek safety from snakes.

A sudden change of crashofwave
draws my attention down
to the foot of the redandgrey lime stonecrumble,
where piratebones make a causeway rise.

From bosunsnecktop, I clamber down
and stumble on the scattered scurvy stoneswalk out.
The landbridge, reveals itself from the surftide,
And the slick granitestones slip my heels
into the birdshitandbarnacle mortar

I, with wetbootheels, step onto the pirateisland.
It is musselsandstones and the beating surf
has not yet crushed it into sand
But my boots and heavy steps do what they can.

The stonebeach is narrow, with only a bare sliver
Between hightideline and cedarthicket
A savagegarden inviolate, primordial
A forest of treasuresandlife grows on pirateisland.
Stranded whitetaildeer and transient birds guard
the interior from lootseekers, but I delve,
ducking lowboughs, giantstreamfording and highstepping roots.

Near the island's westshore, that faces the AtlanticDeep
not on the beach, but close to the saltstones,
a mossgrove rises, greenasdeep as the mossandquiet.
It absorbs my bootheels, like deep pile carpetsponge.

The forestmoss grows on birchesandceders like lichen,
but soft, and unlichen-like carpets the duff.
Nothing moves there except myself,
and I leave what buccaneerbullion I reveal.

This saltstonebeach on the Bay of Fundy,
offers adventuresanddangers and no cause way,
gives soakedboots, and ankletwisting
from a rollingstone my foot found in risingsurf.

Rounding the westshore, a ridge rises. I climb.
Fingertips dig into the limestonechalk,
scrabbletoes find purchase for clambering.
I reach the top dampanddusted, salted.

I standandsee sea meet giantstreammouth
Swirlingcurrent, crashingwaves curling with turbulence.
The riptides hide, but I can see them.
Now I see the giantblood in giantstream, where pirateblade spilled it

GiantStream disappears at PirateGrove and aims across to
BosunsNeckTop atop PirateBones.

Later, I walkedabout again. Another walkingstory.

At Walden Pond

I walked for a time with a chipmunk.
He kept the pace and three feet of safety space from me, possible
                                                        predator.
He had a french fry in his mouth.

I moved suddenly onto a new track,
And startled him,
he fled into the woods and greener fields, and I hope he did better
                                                                                 there.

The late afternoon cool, mottled green light smells of disturbed earth
                                                      and young growth.
I breathe it in and hold it in.

I placed a pebble in tribute to him,
at his house, near a tree, off to the side of the main cairn.
I sat in his house while I wrote this, making a meal for the
                                                                mosquitoes.

Gluttony

I rhyme with
      regular thyme
or parsley
Parsnips.
or cheesy Nips.
Food makes me
      comfortable.
      Happy.

Fool

I am almost fooled
Plastic plants are just as green.
Truth may be there, too.

The root

at the root,
I am sitting at the foot of the Banyan Tree
like Siddartha did, sitting at the root
at the root
looking for the root of it.

even while the thunder
pounds the Carribean sky
even the rain thunders down
at the root,
at the root I cannot sense
that all life is suffering

I cannot believe
that this nest of wood
at the root
at the root is suffering

struggling yes, at the root, for life,
for life to win at the root
at the root
a living sense sends vines to the ground
to make new trunks
to spread the tree to the sky
into the ground
At the root

The healer

He sits, locked in bronze,
arms and legs plainly
resting from carrying the load in
his chest.
His broad-brimmed hat's flair
and the flaring cape
make me smile, then laugh.
A joking, funny older man who touches
his nose to show his humor.

And there is no gate on his heart,
so he can let his patients free,
when they are ready, healed.

statue of a man, sitting

he hardly existed
and his name is forgotten
but his solidity resisted extinction,
his deep-etched laughter, gently falls
around his eyes

the strength of his joyful
serenity seems barely able to hold
his laughter in

Sherwood Island

I am on a rock at the shore, slouching
A granite block, a throne,
on an island, perched high
on a boulder-jetty, in the saltspray
Waves slide like sandpaper over the smaller stoney sounds

I am sitting on an island throne gazing
at Long Island, across the saltfroth
the boats and fathoms between
the shore and the shore
Waves, small across the Sound, making little sound

I wonder if I could see me sitting
on my stone throne
if I gazed at me from there
if I peered across the water,
Waving at myself, would I stand out, over the Sound?

I think the geese would know, and the lobsters crawling,
would they were here.
Here, there are sand fleas,
here, there are seagulls,
Waving in their ways, but they are making hungry sounds.

I, an adult, am treasure-hunting
But there's piracy to fear,
and murdering to bear
and no X to mark the spot.
Waves and children are for finding gold in the Sound

I'm bare-footprinting this well-travelled beach, exploring
to find emeralds of the past
in mother-of-pearl oyster chests
in seaweeds, saltstains and sandcastles
Waves pull at my exposed toes and I hear the ancient sounds

I see a sea of geese, softly in the surf bobbing.

They are a congregation in the shallows
not feeding, only floating
not honking, only drifting or bobbing
Waving gently at each other while I feed the flies by the Sound

I peer at the horizon, home of all adventuring
where the new land always is,
appearing like boats
appearing like voices across and away,
Waving for me with beckons, sirens, faint echoes of sounds.

I want to know where I have to be standing
in order to see
myself at the horizon
myself on the boats and islands at the horizon,
Waves that would be carrying me to me, to the Sound.

watching

The women get ready to go out,
a drink. French and Spanish and
I sit here watching, not going along,
though I don't know why.
I could. The Spaniard is quite friendly,
but I do nothing.
A relationship is impossible, and sex?
Though nice, also impossible.
Too many roommates.
What I need is a moment or two alone. Truly alone,
without people around. Also impossible.
I am isolated, but not alone.

Time

A jackrabbit with staring blue eyes
A newborn at 29 blinks staring awake
A girl with staring black eyes
A doe bounds into the brush, heaving breaths

a pellet is left on the road, steaming
an empty bottle next to a steeping tea
a red pool, foggy with hot steam
a tuft of stray fur snags white against the brush

Mountain

the hot, wet finger of electric
fire races at her
madness of sustained
anticipation gnawing at the edge

almost touching sinking into
flare and boom and
penetration

raw power forcing itself upon her

the tube

what with minding the gap
and staying to the right,
193 steps to the top
at Charing Cross station,
the Underground is a responsibility.

The portrait

He levels his accusative stare
at me. What news was in his letter
that caused him to find fault in me?
Why does he point that gaze at me?
No one else in the room seems to notice
or be bothered, but I, I am stabbed through
by the loss and betrayal and hopeless
venom in the eyes of this man glaring at me.

Shroud

London is shrouded like
a mourning widow
Dark cloth and wildly reaching hair,
but grey and red-eyed at the window
foggy with incomprehension at her loss.

New York subway rat

A rat is dying
in the subway track litter.

It doesn't bleed, dying
among the litter, but it squirms.

And I watch it die
alone among the litter, eventually

leaving the litter behind.

Swim

When I was young, in summer I built dams to keep back the sea.

I piled sand into neolithic mounds, knee-high mountains that towered above the beach. Walls of wet, course granules of ground rock and detritus. Then the tide rose and brushed my walls away like so much sand before the sea.

My wall washed away, and my feet wet and cold, I walked away from the rising sea.

At the next tide, I tried weaving a reef. Driftwood branches and seaweed, I built a barrier. Tight knots and thick wood would hold the tide away. And it held, except. Except the sea found the cracks, slipped inside like a thief or a lover. My feet were wet and my knees cold.

I walked away, away up the beach, away from the creeping sea and it broke my barricade.

At the next tide I dressed for battle. I had learned. I wore hip boots. This time my feet would be dry. I had learned. I constructed better. This time, my reef would be the bones. This time, my mounds would be the skin. This time, black, brittle, hard mussel shells would be armor against the tide.

I watched and waited as the water rose. We were placid, together. Triumph when the terrible bulk pushed the salt away. Crushed when the salt swept it all away, crushed.

I stood and let the tide rise over my toes, my knees. I was not wet. I was not cold. I was dry. I was cold.

I walked away from the rising sea, sloshing in the water, leaving no trace. Feeling no victory.

At the next tide, I went with no boots. No stratagem. No craft. At the next tide, I sat on the sand and watched the sea slip, creep, sweep up the beach. Absent minded, I dug into the sand a small semi-circle in front of me and on the sides. It grew deep. Inches, even.

The tide rolled into my trench, but I didn't worry. Soon it was full, and the saltwater poured over me, over my position. I was in it.

I had no wall, no barricade, no fortress. Only an open moat. I was cold. I was wet. I did not walk away. I reclined into the rolling summer sea and it rocked me gently, like a lover.

So I swam away from the beach.

Firehouse

The beer hall in Albany
has the feel of a municipal building,
a firehouse

This twelve-foot ceiling
is supported by plaster and oak walls,
dark with smoke and time

This room rumbles with chuckling
conversations and smells of malt,
caramel, coffee and this warm brown ale.

Blending beer and warm smells and cool
Autumn air make a heady perfume and heat
like when your skin glows but not with sweat

I could ask the bartender for the history
He's garrulous and congenial and not too busy
To chat with the pretty woman three stools away or with me

I'd rather think about old sleeping bunks
on the upper floor and a tall, brass pole
and three-alarm fires fought four blocks and forty years away

Pub Song

Dark rough-hewn wood
       and candlelight illuminate the bar
And the man next to me is drinking
       professionally, like a man who cares
       Perhaps the stack of twenty dollar bills neatly folded
will buy the answer to the question posed by his wet eyes and sighs.
Twenty or sixty or eighty dollars will not buy him back. Or her.
       It will buy one night of public privacy as the bartender smiles
at him. She knows she can help.

She can help the balding, blond English bloke,
       working hard on the younger woman next to him at the bar.
       He buys her another drink. Chardonnay or Coffee or Beer.

And the two couples at the table next to the Christmas tree try to
       laugh louder than the twenty-somethings chortling at
       urbane, witty jokes. One-upmanship.
Funnier is smarter and they are unaware of the couples,
who are unaware.

But they compete.

And it is early yet.
Seven-thirty and the bar is nearly empty. Monday night.

And the waitress is bored because there are only two tables and
everyone ordered at the bar to get the three dollar drink special.

I notice a lone woman on the last bar stool.
She reads the Times with studied concentration. Her drink stands,
       untouched and she seems not to mind being alone
       with her paper. And I don't think she does mind.

Happy Hour.

The radio is playing Magical Mystery Tour.

The Guinness is creamy and foamy and
        quenching and I need a cigarette.

I come back inside and my refill is waiting and I over tip
        the generous woman behind the bar.

And the laughing couples have left and been replaced
        by an elderly pair. They are not drinking, but ordering food.
        And the waitress seems happy to see them.

And my neighbor has been joined by a man,
        whose striped baby-blue shirt subtly clashes
        with his solid tie in a lighter shade.

It is eight o'clock and happy hour is over and
        I guess I'll finish my beer
The woman with the calm eyes,
        steadily reading day-old cold news
        is still alone, too.

Coffee shops

In coffee shops we gather,
caffeinating our lives
to soft jazz music,
Ella and Nat King Cole,
the sounds of our
grandparents falling in love
and remembering their lives and
searching for their pre-war innocence

In coffee shops we eavesdrop
on neighbors and strangers
to reassure ourselves,
to reaffirm that the
tastes and sounds and smells of
our lives are not less rich than theirs.

In coffee shops we taste
what a bartender can't give
with all his urban wisdom.
We drink in our own truths
with foam and cinnamon,
or black.

In coffee shops we recover
with our chosen families,
new bonds forged to sear away
the wounds of dysfunctionality.

In coffee shops we find
the methodology of survival
in the eye of our hurricane lives,
the winds held at bay by espresso
and decaf and company.

Upon the celebration of a decade together: a Story.

The story of my life is made of words;
sentences strung into tales, wound in verbs,
people and places, and adjectives and gerunds that come and go.
But now, at this moment I am deep, darkly groping
as I soak my mind within a decade, to know
the story of ten years in only a few words.

You, you who own ten years of mine, deserve
not merely words. But they are all I have.
So they are yours, too.

I've written you, and for you, many times.
Sometimes the lines come like soft, dark chocolate from my mind.
Some times, like the time I have here, stretch as a decade on the line.
And the words have always come, for you.
I think about our decade together and I can't tell one, our story.
There are so many Scheherazades that could pour from me.
The liquor of our life has been so rich and we always drank,
however heady.

You drank for me, and I for you.

You, you who own ten years of mine, deserve
all my mere words. Because they are all I have.
And they are yours, too.

The words are there, are yours.
The story is there, is ours.
We tell a tale of adventures in fire,
and soaking and drinking and singing the waters entirely.
Not without fear, but never without us, entire.
And in ten years, I have loved being yours.

You, you who own ten years of mine, own all
these words of mine, because they, and I, are all I have.
And we are yours, too.

Mythology

Paris could not have seen in Helen
when he stole the gem of Sparta
what I can see in her.
Eyes and feet and flat stomach
like an Aegean statue,
risen from the wet ocean fog
like Aphrodite from the foam.

And like Hera, hardly trusting,
never secure in her Zeus' word
searching for an Orphean lover.
Music and magic and great deeds
and none of Mycenae.
She is the reflection of a nymph.

When the storm heaves up
the surface of the ocean,
before the gale comes to
lash the frothy waves,
like this she swells me.

Changeling

You changeling —
You never stop searing
my expectations away
Like a prestidigitator working
in a podunk backwater town
who makes magic in sceptical minds

So do you astonish me.

breathing

I draw in breath, wide open mouth
a breath of the breadth of the earth,
tasting of my beagle
and humid summer air.

I draw deep, deep inhaling
the hot dark wine
of an August evening,
hearing young teenagers playing
football in the street, blind.

My pores open to the moist,
drinking the liquid night
into me, refreshing
my body and blood.

Too soon I exhale,
adding my heat to the air,
my breath and dampness
changing it slightly,
warming it silently.

I inhale again, again deep
and rich the flavor of the
New England late summer air.
Waiting, holding my breath
before another exhalation into
autumnal clarity.

Alone

Alone I am.
But not lonesome.
shadows and things
even less tangible
enjoy my company.

As do birds,
airborne travelers
and
iron creatures
wasting away their lazy
comfort.

Sound also,
song and hum
soaring through the heavens
and creeping on the
concrete.

Perhaps I am not alone at all.

Memorial

The people are so small, who mourn here
Mourning are the beech stretching beyond view, high and deep
The ground is dark, umber; flower patches strewn about.
No one weeps. No tearing on dun fabric, charcoal gray and black

Only the wind speaks, whispering the elegy
The people are so small, who grieve here.

Dawn at the Great Pyramid

Serpentine horns spit like reptilian weeping
at the Egyptians at dawn.
And the Drums beat them from sleeping.

In language old with god-kings,
the people sing at dawn.
And serpentine horns spit like reptilian weeping

at cool-breezed beauty in desert burning
sands. Sahara and Nile waters yawn
and the Drums beat them from sleeping

in the coolness before the heat of flaming
sky. Copper is in color and scent and thickness drawn
and serpentine horns spit like reptilian weeping

at the infrared rainbow arching
over Khufu's tomb at dawn.
And the Drums beat them from sleeping,

And the children laugh while dew is drying,
And they stretch and yawn,
And serpentine horns spit like reptilian weeping,
And the drums beat them from sleeping.

Chicken story

I don't dislike chickens
      or birds at all
           Nor am I immune to Salmonella,
                probably.

But the facts should never limit the scope of a good story,
        leave it mundane. Leave it extraordinary.

Simple life is nice. Stories start there,
        but the ones I like grow from that seed of normalcy.
        The seed of the banal can grow into an improbable tree
            of impossibilities

Wrestling a bear or winning a duel for honor or rolling a car
fifteen times and walking away or killing for money as a youth

or becoming immune to disease
        to oppose the oncoming poultry potentate

Journey

Walk with me
Talk with me
Share with me
a mile -
If you tell me a joke,
I might give you a smile
We might be friends
      through prosper and thin -

Or maybe only until the desert begins -

But whether or not
      we companions will stay -
I'm glad to have known you
That we passed by the way -

meeting

I do not know her, but I like her.
She is moving out of my life
and, I expect, for good,
but she rumbles me tonight
like hunger and I want
to satisfy myself.

I have enjoyed the little
exchanges of body language,
intimate, seemingly accidental, touches
on arms or back or hair
and the casualesque conversation

Hearth

I see a flaming love-seat
        and the heat
                of the stroke and the brush
                          is palpable

Lord of the Dance

Shiva Nataraja stands poised
while chaos spins dance in the void
        but Lord of this Dance
        breathes courage and stands
as his hair is pulled in the noise.

Shiva Dances with balance
on the back of prostrate ignorance
        hands hold life and death
        man and woman's breath
as His sash is torn off, He cries, "Dance."

Pollock

He has passion, this man,
a fire in his mind that burns
him and splashes out on canvas.
Magma from the great Pollock fault.

His mind burns, but his soul is cool
with strong borders in grey and
black, tempering the red and yellow
and orange lake trying to shatter
and his soul is twisting,
toiling not to crack.

Holding fiercely, still, in summer.

float

Lady Luna, gliding like an
iceberg across the sea of stars
You turn a deaf ear to my pleadings
you refuse to hear my tears

Like a river flows my grieving
soul away and You do nothing
Floating has grown so difficult
as my lost love, a stone, drags me under

Reflection

In the rearview mirror
        the crystalline
        reflection of
a left hand
holding a nonchalant cigarette
        between fingers
that sport a claddagh
        worn by someone in love.
And then a butterfly fluttered by,
        a yellow one
and the liquid smoke
        sparkled as it slid away

Sloth

Birds are singing at the edge of the sea,
      watching the smouldering sunset with me

Lovers are frothing the edge of the sea,
      silly and splashing the surf, merrily

The sun is skilled at setting, seducing
      setting we sitters in salaciousness

You

I like how you walk
        and breathe
and don't wear shoes on your bed to humor me
You don't mind.

You lie like a rug on the floor
In a fuzzy, soft, not cold on my bare feet kind of way.

Hunting

Satyrs and wolves and bears and men
        and only the satyrs are armed
The fires rage, tearing down the wilds
        gnashing, preying, viscous chaos
Very close to the front, two men try
        to pry two dogs off a bleeding screaming bear.
And a satyr, face serene prepares to bring
        his twisted cudgel down
upon them.

Frozen

In the blooming union of these two,
passion held with reddened faces
and yet to be cast away traces
of clothes of gold and white and blue.

Artfully crafted word and flower
seducing even cherubim.
She holds her breath and she waits for him,
and he reaches out to touch her.

Too quickly pass the summer's graces,
hours spent in unchaste longing
on the long-vanished granite fountain.

Unfulfilled, tangled limb with limb,
a fever built through long embracing
and knowing moistened lips must meet.

Scavengers

The seagulls swarming
        angry hornets
        at the trash
A child asks her mother
        about another leftover
        dinner.
She wears a beekeeper suit shopping
        and they wheel their cart home.
Home.
And she asks if they are there
        yet.
Soon.
When?
Soon.
Tell me about Daddy.

And a story about a man
        with rocky fists.
A fairy tale about a fiction
who died a hero in the war.
And is he in heaven?
Yes

Because here is not and
        he is not here.
I love you.
And the girl's mother wipes away
        her windy tears and
        the gulls dive and claw
        for scraps to feed
hungry chicks.
Tearing life from left overs.

Lust

The creepycrawlies
I get from his
touch
Thrill me with satisfaction.

She chills me
bone shivers with
heat
And I cannot quite breathe.

untitled(wedding)

In the early hours of a freezing morning our two roads converged,
and that fusion of a moment paved
a wide, tree-lined avenue in silver and copper.

It released a furnace blast, out of proportion to the plain crossroads.
In that alchemical instant, however, a new future began.

untitled(notice)

Notice the way the horizon
      glows
            long after the sun falls
into the next hemisphere, there is purple left behind
        a deep kind with indigo and void
    black
the way the horizon disappears

Missing

New England hangs off the edge of the continent in early autumn
Like the rusted bumper of an old Ford Deuce
Like an old woman's hand on a windowsill,
                                      etched with deep lines and blue veins
Like a teenager, out of her bedroom, as her friends sail by.

Pride

There is just so much sky
so much pale blue and cloud and
the powers, the works of men are so small

My Sacrificial Lamb

My sacrificial lamb
is a naughty little sheep.
But it is mine and warm.

Everyone wants me to give up my sheep.
I'll miss the good times with my fluffy friend.
If I agree to this.

My fortune-teller says I should.
So does my family and wallet and god.
And my nerves

My sheep was warm and mine.
Now it is just warm and missed.
I have lost. And loved.

oliver cromwell

As I stand before the statue
of oliver cromwell,
Lord Protector of England,
the murderer,
I am struck because
everyone seems to know

I spit on the ground
near his memorial at Parliament
because I respect Westminster
too much to spit on his grave and
I can't get close enough to piss on the statue.

Sirensong

The breakers are grinding stones down
granite and limestones are satin to the breaking surf

It froths right before it bites

Behind the froth rides a calmer face,
not sedate -- but less frothy.
This countenance swells
before it expels the frothy waves
to grind the stones
that will in an eon be sand.

Still farther out
there is another gazer.
She stares at the shore with longing and simmering loathing
and goes still
only when she fixates on a new sensation.
She waits and digests and then, then simmers again.

That is where the sirens live.
On the deep rocks
where shore is near enough to see,
but far enough that there is no safety,
yet,
from the seething,
swelling,
frothing,
hungered sea.

There in the deeper water where danger lurks,
the sirens call.

They sing sweetly, but softly,
but sultry

they promise

and to those sailors who beach safely they will deliver
but few can find a berth
on the sirens' beach.

There, on top of razor cliffs that stubbornly refuse to be ground down,
they call.

Lyrics that seduce their sailors close

There above the spears of stone,
jutting out of the
deep water,
they grow calm only when digesting
or waiting

Soon they will simmer again.
And swell.
And sing.

And the unsuspecting sailor swells and begins to froth
and gnaw on his bindings.

And I wanted to find a berth, but I found a siren
And she sings and we feast and simmer and sometimes
grow still.

The Spaniard

Not just one, but The One
—a heavy load
maybe that's why all the people
are squiggly and weighed down
and the sky over Toledo is heavy,
dark with clouds.

Dark Water

Grey, even in summer,
        especially before and directly after a storm.
        Dark Atlantic water.

Steel, with a temper giving it shine when light strikes
        obliquely just right in the morning and at dusk
        evoking the bell it could sound like,
        if you knew how best to strike it —

a tone that would break your heart at the sorrow in it
        or soften your heart to the sorrows upon it
        or swell your spirit.

After a storm, or on a rare, clear, cloudless day,
        some times the sun strikes slate Atlantic eyes
                                  far off the coast,
        far from the beaches and far from the rocks, the water peals
                                  joyous notes,
        peels off its grey frock to don a cerulean gown,

and seems to draw up at the corners in a smile.

The wind is speaking

There is a storm tonight —
The bad kind.

A northeast wind is pushing the storm,
bending the softwoods and cracking oak
and elm and maple branches

and this wind calls for a fist raised in the dark
and it calls out their names into the light

A liar is masked as a madman,
a buffoon in the role of a leader
is a liar, telling lies

The gale is fighting the storm,
it is the good kind
It is moving the storm and it is the wind of

Voices that have always been there
and now will be heard
screaming their names
carried on the wind
driving the storm away

It is the best kind of wind.
It clears the storm.
It brings the light after it.

It speaks the names.

Eulogy for a woman I did not know

It doesn't seem real,
but my eyes fill
looking at the woman who lies
dying alone. She is mourned
by a young, soft-footed boy and
a dog with ears and eyes
and tail heavy. But still she
lies alone as her last moments
drain upon the ground and everything
else just continues, regardless.

Eliot (a reply)

We are not empty
we fill our lives,
such as we make them.
I defy your pessimism.
I will not allow you to
condescend
to show me your abject
hopelessness
Stop giving me your despair

like bile.

dream

silence creeping
darkness weeping
lying in my sheets at night
sweating
don't know if i'm dreaming
can't tell if it's true
can't tell if it happened
can't tell if i was there
can't tell anymore.
i don't know why
it's this way
i don't know if i could say
it's going now.
good
night -

the fire and the water

      the great beast
consumes and
      demands feeding
crying out its
      hunger, aching to be
satiated.

      unknowing that
just as it exists to devour
      creeping, patient in its age
approaches one who lives
      only to consume
           the Fire

slowly it comes,
      engulfing all it touches
using everything
      in its inexorable need

      the fire fights its ancient foe
onward the enemy creeps
      bravely it flares and heats
devouring more and more

onward the enemy creeps

      with a great bellow of pain,
          it is finished
by the rolling
      soaking
      aching
hunger of
          the Water

Act I, scene 1

close
gap
between
when I fall
&
talking

Start
on the ground

a seduction

with a voice that
liquefied glass he asked
for my name.
And I told him I was

Azriel

An angel, he called me.
Nervous, I chose a
cloven cigarette.
He offered me a light,
which I took.
That night I fell,

with him.

Easy showers

The way it rains in New Orleans
in the cheap air of summer
is like a well-staged fight

It is violent in appearance,
and the area clears, except
for the few combatants

Everyone is dripping wet
with rain or heavy sweat
moving fast and looking slow

Dodge from safety to cover
through danger or downpour
And there is little harm, except

the kiss

cool, forbidden,
clandestine theft of
just one moment together
secretly, silently calculated to burn

the struggle

Sweaty arms wrap me
around in
he attempts to knock me
down up
I latch on and pull his
weight down on
me him
We fall and he pins me

Victory

under the
floor of the house
live goblins

grabbing
grappling for purchase
on my ankle

but I evade them
and I mock them

as I run away as fast as I can

untitled(boy in a sweatshirt)

a boy in a red plaid sweatshirt,
grey brain with little to do
but ooze.
his brain drips rich, thick thoughts,
mine softly murmurs
ideas and inventions
and I pour them
       into you

Dreamers

Even horses dream of other horses
    blue and red with green
        exclamations

    In horses' dreams, people are
        round and square with flat
            features

        And orchids' dreams are
            colors and shapes and deep
                pollination

Justine

Irrespective of her quill and curls,
her carefully tied back hair, demurely
draped gown and
Halo;

St Justine seems to glance at me
like a woman
with desires only a pagan god could
Satisfy.

Musician

great, huge Gouges through the
        silent air and canvas.

this man plays with Fury
        painted fast as he was;

fingers Rippling o'er keys
        between and through the cubes.

Night feather edges find
        hard, dark inner music.

surprise

I sprint
          eager
          to see
                    her
                            show

carefully
sneaking in
seating in
the back

                            I leave,
          eager
          to surprise
     her
after

symbols

Fresh baked bread
eggs, scrambled
sizzling bacon fat
    footy pajamas
    my favorite fork
    late morning

Chunky peanut butter and marmalade
Milk, whole
Bartlett pear slices
    dripping through my fingers
    cold on my teeth
    cut with the big knife

New York sirloin steak
onions, sautéed
salt and butter in mashed potatoes
    cooked rare and bloody enough
        mash on top like dad makes it
    or smashed potatoes, I like it

Notebook

In my book I look for images
of poems in trees and trays of fruit,
still-lives on paper in ink
verbal geometry, concrete as
a speaker phone, muted carefully with
humming dial tone and buzzing off the hook
on the other end. I try to make more sense
out of random ideas and sounds assaulting
my ears and eyes. Color owns my brain on
autumn days and silver-washed pregnant nights
or oil-streaked rainbow crows and brighter
chromium fenders filling my mouth with tinfoil,
tasting fruit flavors. And other times I smell
baking meatloaf and fumes from paint
and car exhaust and not just those, but pre-snow
dryness, air that broods, heavy.

ABOUT THE AUTHOR

Ken Briodagh is a storyteller, writer and editor and founder of StoryPhoenix.com. He's a piratical, poetic, paternal, polyamorous, partial alliterist. You can find him on Twitter @AtlasWriter and everywhere else with Google. His SEO is great.

In previous lives, he's been a short order cook, telemarketer, medical supply technician and mover of the bodies at a funeral home. Most of his exploits are either exaggerated or blatantly false and he's just as glad no one can prove otherwise.

He lives in New England, if that wasn't obvious.

Made in the USA
Middletown, DE
30 March 2024